THIS BOOK BELONGS TO

_____

FOR THE KIDS WHO WANT TO HELP

ISBN: 9798894581927

IN A QUIET LITTLE VILLAGE, SNOWFLAKES DANCED IN THE CHILLY DECEMBER AIR. EVERYONE WAS BUSY PREPARING FOR CHRISTMAS, EXCEPT FOR YOUNG CLARA.

CLARA LOVED CHRISTMAS, BUT THIS YEAR FELT DIFFERENT. HER FAMILY HAD LITTLE MONEY, AND SHE WORRIED THERE WOULD BE NO GIFTS UNDER THE TREE.

ONE FROSTY MORNING, CLARA FOUND AN OLD PAIR OF BOOTS SITTING BY THE TOWN FOUNTAIN.
THEY SPARKLED FAINTLY, AS IF TOUCHED BY MAGIC.

CURIOUS, CLARA SLIPPED HER FEET INTO THE BOOTS. THEY FIT PERFECTLY, AND THE WORLD AROUND HER SEEMED TO SHIMMER.

A GENTLE VOICE WHISPERED, "THESE ARE THE GIVING BOOTS. THEY HELP THOSE WHO WEAR THEM SPREAD KINDNESS AND JOY."

CLARA WAS ASTONISHED. SHE LOOKED AROUND, WONDERING HOW SHE COULD USE
THE BOOTS. THEN, SHE SAW MR. TURNER, THE BAKER, LOOKING SAD.

"MR. TURNER, ARE YOU ALRIGHT?" CLARA ASKED. HE SIGHED, "I'VE RUN OUT OF SUGAR AND CAN'T BAKE GINGERBREAD FOR THE CHILDREN."

CLARA'S BOOTS SPARKLED. SHE FOUND HERSELF RUNNING TO HER PANTRY AT HOME, GATHERING THE LAST BIT OF SUGAR HER FAMILY HAD.

"HERE, MR. TURNER," CLARA SAID, HANDING HIM THE SUGAR. HIS FACE LIT UP.
"THANK YOU, CLARA! YOU'VE SAVED CHRISTMAS FOR MANY!"

AS SHE WALKED HOME, CLARA NOTICED THE BOOTS GLOWING BRIGHTER.
SHE REALIZED THEY GREW MORE MAGICAL WITH EACH ACT OF KINDNESS.

THE NEXT DAY, CLARA SAW MRS. HANSON SHIVERING ON HER PORCH. HER COAT WAS OLD AND FULL OF HOLES.

CLARA'S BOOTS GLIMMERED, AND SHE HURRIED HOME TO FIND HER EXTRA SCARF. "HERE, MRS. HANSON. THIS WILL KEEP YOU WARM," CLARA SAID.

Mrs Hanson:

"You're a blessing, Clara."

MRS. HANSON SMILED WARMLY. "YOU'RE A BLESSING, CLARA." THE BOOTS SHONE EVEN MORE, FILLING CLARA'S HEART WITH WARMTH.

WORD OF CLARA'S KINDNESS SPREAD THROUGH THE VILLAGE. PEOPLE BEGAN TO SMILE MORE,
AND THE SPIRIT OF CHRISTMAS GREW STRONGER.

ONE EVENING, CLARA SAW LITTLE BEN CRYING BY THE TOWN SQUARE. "WHAT'S WRONG, BEN?" SHE ASKED GENTLY.

"I LOST MY WOODEN TRAIN," BEN SOBBED. "IT WAS MY ONLY TOY." THE BOOTS TWINKLED, URGING CLARA TO ACT.

CLARA REMEMBERED HER OWN TOY CHEST. SHE PICKED OUT HER FAVORITE STUFFED
BEAR AND BROUGHT IT TO BEN.

"HERE, BEN," SHE SAID. "THIS BEAR WILL KEEP YOU COMPANY." BEN'S EYES LIT UP AS HE HUGGED THE BEAR TIGHTLY.

The Giving Boots

THE GIVING BOOTS GLOWED LIKE NEVER BEFORE. CLARA REALIZED THAT KINDNESS DIDN'T NEED TO BE GRAND; EVEN SMALL ACTS MADE A DIFFERENCE.

THE DAYS PASSED, AND CLARA CONTINUED SPREADING KINDNESS. SHE HELPED CARRY FIREWOOD, SHARED HER BREAD, AND SANG CAROLS TO THE LONELY.

ON CHRISTMAS EVE, THE BOOTS LED CLARA TO THE VILLAGE CHURCH, WHERE THE T OWNSPEOPLE WERE GATHERING FOR A SPECIAL CELEBRATION.

INSIDE, A LARGE TREE STOOD IN THE CENTER, BARE AND UNDECORATED. THE VILLAGERS LOOKED PUZZLED. "WE'VE RUN OUT OF ORNAMENTS," SOMEONE SAID.

THE BOOTS SPARKLED BRIGHTER THAN EVER. CLARA HAD AN IDEA. SHE RUSHED HOME AND GATHERED RIBBONS, BUTTONS, AND BITS OF FABRIC.

"LET'S DECORATE WITH WHAT WE HAVE!" CLARA SAID, SHARING HER TREASURES. THE VILLAGERS JOINED IN, CRAFTING ORNAMENTS FROM SIMPLE ITEMS.

WHEN THE TREE WAS COMPLETE, IT SPARKLED WITH HOMEMADE DECORATIONS.
EVERYONE AGREED IT WAS THE MOST BEAUTIFUL TREE THEY HAD EVER SEEN.

AS THE VILLAGERS SANG CAROLS, THE GIVING BOOTS BEGAN TO GLOW SOFTLY. CLARA
FELT A DEEP SENSE OF JOY AND PEACE.

THE GENTLE VOICE RETURNED. "YOU HAVE USED THE BOOTS WELL, CLARA.
THEY'VE TAUGHT YOU THAT THE GREATEST GIFT IS KINDNESS."

CLARA LOOKED DOWN AND SAW THE BOOTS FADING INTO THE SNOW. SHE DIDN'T FEEL SAD;
THEIR MAGIC NOW LIVED IN HER HEART.

FROM THAT CHRISTMAS ON, CLARA INSPIRED THE VILLAGE TO GIVE AND SHARE,
EVEN WITHOUT THE MAGICAL BOOTS.

EVERY ACT OF KINDNESS, NO MATTER HOW SMALL, BECAME THE NEW
TRADITION OF THE LITTLE VILLAGE.

AND EACH YEAR, THE VILLAGERS WOULD GATHER BY THE TREE, REMEMBERING HOW ONE GIRL AND A PAIR OF BOOTS CHANGED THEIR LIVES.

CLARA NEVER FORGOT THE GIVING BOOTS. THOUGH THEY DISAPPEARED,
SHE KNEW THEIR MAGIC WAS IN EVERY KIND ACT.

CHRISTMAS WASN'T ABOUT GIFTS OR DECORATIONS, CLARA REALIZED. IT WAS ABOUT LOVE, KINDNESS, AND THE JOY OF GIVING.

AS SNOW FELL GENTLY, CLARA WHISPERED, "THANK YOU, GIVING BOOTS, FOR TEACHING ME THE TRUE SPIRIT OF CHRISTMAS."

The Villlage

THE VILLAGE SPARKLED WITH JOY, LAUGHTER, AND THE WARMTH OF
TOGETHERNESS. CLARA'S HEART GLOWED BRIGHTER THAN EVER.

EACH SNOWFLAKE SEEMED TO CARRY THE MAGIC OF KINDNESS, SPREADING
IT FAR BEYOND THE LITTLE VILLAGE.

AND SO, THE GIVING BOOTS' STORY BECAME A LEGEND, REMINDING EVERYONE TO GIVE FROM THE HEART.

CHILDREN WOULD SIT BY THE FIRE, LISTENING TO THE TALE OF THE BOOTS AND DREAMING OF SPREADING KINDNESS THEMSELVES.

THE SPIRIT OF THE GIVING BOOTS LIVED ON, IN EVERY SMILE,
EVERY HUG, AND EVERY ACT OF LOVE.

AND IN THE QUIET LITTLE VILLAGE, CHRISTMAS WAS FOREVER BRIGHT,
THANKS TO CLARA AND HER GIVING BOOTS.

I HOPE YOU LIKED THIS BOOK

www.ingramcontent.com/pod-product-compliance
Lightning Source LLC
Chambersburg PA
CBHW081540120626
46550CB00009B/2813

* 9 7 9 8 8 9 4 5 8 1 9 2 7 *